It's Easy to Fake...
Acoustic Guitar

by Joe Bennett

Exclusive Distributors:
Music Sales Corporation
257 Park Avenue South, New York, NY10010, USA.
Music Sales Limited
8/9 Frith Street, London W1D 3JB, England.
Music Sales Pty Limited
120 Rothschild Avenue, Rosebery, NSW 2018, Australia.

Order No. AM 973786
ISBN 0.8256.1929.7
This book © Copyright 2002 Amsco Publications

Written by Joe Bennett.
Edited by Sorcha Armstrong.
Musical examples by Richard Barrett.
Music engraving by Digital Music Art.

Book design by Phil Gambrill.
Cover design by Michael Bell Design.
Illustrations by Andy Hammond.

Specialist guitar pictures supplied courtesy of
Balafon Books (pages 8, 89-91 and 93)
Text photographs courtesy of London Features International and Redferns.
Chord photographs (pages 30-35) by George Taylor.

Printed in the United States of America by
Vicks Lithograph and Printing Corporation

www.musicsales.com

It's Easy to Fake...
Acoustic Guitar

by Joe Bennett

Amsco Publications
London / New York / Paris / Sydney / Copenhagen / Madrid / Tokyo

Introduction 7
The Story of the Acoustic Guitar 8
The Players...

Bluffers Chords 30
Music and TAB Guide 36
The Music...

Music Shop Classic 83
Music Shop Riffs 87
Guitars...

Unplugged? 92
Acoustic Light-Bulb Jokes 94
Outro 95

Introduction

Electric guitar players have it too easy, don't they? They just plug in, turn everything up to '11', then stomp on the latest Japanese talent-booster effects pedal. Hey presto — instant Pink Floyd. That's all very well, but what do guitarists do when they're sat under the stars with nothing but a bottle of beer and a Martin D-28?

The whole problem with acoustic guitar is that everyone can hear it. Hit a wrong note on your electric and you can bend it up until it sounds OK, or hit the whammy bar to turn a musical mistake into a Jimi Hendrix reference. On acoustic the note stays where it is, for all to enjoy. This makes it one of the most difficult instruments to bluff with. However, help is at hand.

It's Easy to Fake... Acoustic Guitar shows you how you can fake your way through the cruellest campfire sessions and the fiercest folk clubs with a little knowledge and a few simple tricks. As long as you name-drop the right albums, talk about the right players and know which songs you should be playing, your status as an aficionado of all things acoustic is assured. Keep this book with you at all times, but don't let other people see it — you wouldn't want anyone to find out that you're just faking...

"What, No Classical?"

You may be surprised to see a distinct lack of references to the classical guitar and its players in this book. That's because, in terms of construction and musical style, it's a totally different instrument from the 'acoustic' steel-string. The main differences are:

- **The classical guitar uses nylon strings (even the 'metal' ones are in fact nylon with a metal winding round the outside).**
- The steel (or steel/bronze wound) acoustic guitar strings produce more tension, so the acoustic guitar needs a 'truss rod' — a metal bar going up the inside of the neck to prevent it from bending or breaking.
- **The steel string guitar is usually louder and has more sustain, due to the increased tension, truss rod and metal strings.**
- Classical guitars are generally easier to play due to the lower string tension.
- **Classical guitars are almost never played using a pick.**
- Vibrato and strumming techniques are different due to string materials.
- **Classical players very rarely use alternate tunings apart from dropped D.**
- The acoustic steel-string has a rounded 'radius' to its fingerboard (the classical guitar has a flat fingerboard), which is one of the reasons why you've never heard bottleneck classical guitar!

The Story of the Acoustic Guitar
or 'Who to name-drop, and when'

Although classical guitars have been around for centuries, the steel-string acoustic has only been with us for 150 years or so. For, all intents and purposes, the instrument started with the American Martin company in the 1850s.

You will hear true acoustic trainspotters mention **Lyon** and **Healy** (responsible for the Washburn brand), and of course **Gibson** (who made some of the earliest f-hole acoustics) but basically, if you want to name drop guitar-makers, **C F Martin**'s the man. The company is still making guitars today, and its reputation hasn't dwindled — you'll still see these instruments in the hands of top folk, rock and country players the world over.

However, if you do get accidentally stranded between two acoustic wild bores in their native habitat, you might wish to aid your escape by also mentioning **Gretsch** (early 12-string maker) and perhaps **National/Dobro** (whose guitars featured a metal dish in the centre to amplify the sound). And by the time you've brought up the subject of 1930s **Maccaferri** jazz guitars, you'll probably have made it as far as the door anyway.

The Players

Of course, the only guitarists that any of us can say we've heard are from this century, because no-one was recording before then (you'd think some bright spark record producer would have seen the sense in getting some of those early players down on tape, but maybe CD manufacture was too expensive back in the 19th Century!).

Bluffer's rule #1:
You play acoustic, your dream guitar is a Martin

With this in mind, your first points of reference have to be the early blues players. Many less experienced bluffers will try to name-check the legendary **Robert Johnson** as an early acoustic blues player, but remember that there was literally a generation of players before him. **Blind Blake**, **Charley Patton** and **Blind Lemon Jefferson**'s recordings all pre-dated Johnson, so mentioning their names in the right company guarantees an air of authority.

Above: c.1850 Martin 'Stauffer' with curly headstock and abalone inlay

Acoustic Jazz and the Teddy Bunn clause

Bluffer's rule #2: Use the Teddy Bunn clause when in difficulty — no-one will be able to challenge you.

As the 20s and 30s wore on, jazz guitar became increasingly popular, and like it or loathe it, you can't say you know your acoustic roots unless you're familiar with some of the early jazzers.

Many people know about **Django Reinhardt**, but how about **Lonnie Johnson** or **George Van Eps**? Don't worry yourself with details, though — you can get by with very little knowledge of these people.

Luckily for the acoustic bluffer, all of the early acoustic jazz players had a similar career — single-note acoustic soloing was combined with tasteful rhythm work, but recognition of their talent was limited by the fact that the instrument wasn't amplified. Even more conveniently, you'll find that very few guitarists actually own a recording by acoustic jazz pioneer **Teddy Bunn**.

Thus, you can achieve mastery of any conversation instantly by saying something like "well, you've got to give it to **Reinhardt**, but his tracks just didn't have the unique timing of those early **Teddy Bunn** recordings." Like all the best bluffs, it demonstrates your encyclopedic knowledge while making you impossible to challenge.

First folk and classic country

The earliest country guitarist you need to know about is Maybelle Carter. In the 1930s she invented the technique called 'Carter picking' (so it was just as well she had the same surname...) which consists of picking the melody on the bass strings while strumming chord accompaniment in the gaps between notes.

The next most significant, in technique terms, is undoubtedly **Chet Atkins**. His thumb-and-three-fingers technique has since acted as a blueprint for thousands of acoustic fingerstyle players.

The earliest British folkie you'll hear mentioned is probably **Davey Graham**. As well as inventing the DADGAD acoustic tuning in the 1950s, he also penned the classic instrumental 'Angie', but more importantly laid the groundwork for the many players that followed — **John Renbourn**, **Gordon Giltrap**, **Leo Kottke** and **Bert Jansch** to name but four.

Lots of people who couldn't play guitar very well but got away with it because they had some good songs.

In the mid 1960s, a whole bunch of players arrived who did nothing but strum three chords. While any guitarist would be hard-pushed to call these people an 'influence' on their technique, you'll find that theirs are among the songs you'll be asked to play most often.

So make sure you've got a smattering of **Bob Dylan**, **Neil Young**, **Joan Baez**, **Don McLean** and **Leonard Cohen**. Shouldn't take you too long to learn the material.

Bluffer's rule #3: If your songwriting's any good, no-one will notice your limitations as an acoustic guitarist.

The Fingerpickers

The late 60s and early 70s were something of a heyday for the acoustic guitar. Songwriters like Paul Simon, Joni Mitchell, Donovan and even The Beatles were using an alternating thumb technique based loosely on Chet Atkins' style, and writing material using the guitar as the sole or primary accompaniment.

Pretty much every acoustic guitarist has played their songs at one time or another, so if you haven't got a transcription of **Paul Simon**'s 'The Boxer' or **Joni Mitchell**'s 'The Circle Game', now would be a good time to put things right.

Bluffer's rule #4: It's OK to play acoustic even if you're really a rocker at heart...

Conversely, things looked pretty bad for acoustic players in the 1980s. Synthesizers and electric guitars reigned supreme, and it seemed that people cared more about hairstyles than hammer-ons. It was left to a few brave souls to save the day, and they did, in a spectacular fashion.

A stream of virtuoso players appeared, including **Michael Hedges**, **Adrian Legg** and **Al Di Meola**. If you're brave you might want to check out their recordings, but if you want to learn their material, might I suggest a ten-year vacation and an island retreat?

The Unplugged Generation

These days, thanks partly to one MTV show, acoustic guitar is reigning supreme again. It seems any artist, however noisy their music, can gain instant cred by doing acoustic versions of their songs (although the acclaimed 'Nirvana Unplugged' session, bizarrely, featured an electric guitar through a fuzz pedal).

Even the angry young men of yesteryear have now settled down with pipe, slippers and acoustic flat-top; remember that **Paul Weller** was practically a punk in his Jam days, and **Eric Clapton** was in one of the 60s' loudest, heaviest rock bands.

Bluffer's rule #5: ...and when you get old, you can always retire to MTV.

Fake your way

So there you have it — a brief history of the instrument.

If you remember half of what's written here, it's probably more faking material than you'll need to use in a lifetime. And remember, if another player name-drops someone who doesn't appear in this book, just ask them what they think of **Teddy Bunn**. Works every time.

The Players

Bite-size bios

In this section you'll find an instant guide to six top acoustic guitarists. Remember that these aren't necessarily the most 'important' players, but they are the most 'significant' (i.e. these are the ones to mention if you want to impress people!).

For each artist, I've included some basic **biography** information, notes on **playing style**, plus, more importantly, which **techniques** you should steal in order to facilitate your acoustic career. Of course, you have to know the guitar they used — acoustic guitar aficionados are everywhere and could pounce at any time.

To save you from having to wade through a truckload of CDs, I've also picked out one **essential album** for you to mention (not necessarily the best-known — it can sometimes pay dividends to fake your way by showing you listen to the obscure stuff). If you're actually asked to prove that you've heard the artist, you'd be stuck without the quick and easy '**finest moment**' reference, and you'll find it helpful to casually mention your handy '**knowledgeable fact**'.

Finally, it's always useful to have a few oven-ready opinions up your sleeve. For each player, I've included an 'instant opinion' (usually ambiguous enough to cover all situations) and an 'acceptable criticism'. If you're cool enough to criticize one of the greats, you can consider your acoustic acumen to be truly foolproof.

Chet Atkins CGP

HISTORY AND BACKGROUND:
Born June 20th 1924, Tennessee, USA. Started playing fiddle in country bands while still at school, but soon moved to guitar. His advanced thumb-and-three-fingers technique meant that he could create whole arrangements with bassline, chords and melody on one instrument. After a string of successful albums he went into A&R for RCA records, so he was instrumental (ahem) in launching the careers of **Elvis Presley**, **The Everly Brothers** and **Jim Reeves**, among others. One of the few acoustic guitarists to have consistent top 40 success purely with instrumentals. Added the initials CGP ('Certified Guitar Player') to his name in 1983.

PLAYING STYLE:
Thumb (or thumbpick) covers the bass notes, playing two or four to the bar, while the fingers take the melody. Even if he uses a backing band, the basic idea is the same. Some hits feature the thumb straying onto the top strings occasionally.

TECHNIQUES TO STEAL:
If you play any fingerstyle at all, the odds are that you're indirectly influenced by this man. If you can get your hand round some basic alternating thumb techniques, you're doing pretty well, but listen for some pyrotechnic stuff too. Our Chet uses banjo rolls (fast melodic runs created across several

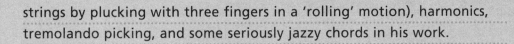

strings by plucking with three fingers in a 'rolling' motion), harmonics, tremolando picking, and some seriously jazzy chords in his work.

GUITARS:
Although his technique suits acoustic so well, we've seen a variety of guitars in the Atkins arsenal. For years he was a Gretsch semi-acoustic endorsee (he now says they "sounded like they were made out of orange boxes") but acoustic-wise he's always been a Gibson man, having recorded with a thin-bodied electro-classical and a Country & Western flat-top.

ESSENTIAL ALBUM:
1975's *Chester And Lester*, a duet with Les Paul, was a massive success, and does contain some great playing, but you'll give yourself several years of study if you just buy any compilation of his '50s and '60s RCA recordings.

FINEST MOMENT:
His famous arrangement of 'The Entertainer' is a great crowd-pleaser, as is his detuned version of 'Vincent', but you can't beat the simplicity of his own tune 'Maybelle' — standard tuning, open C and bar G7 chords, and a country melody to die for. And it was written about country picking pioneer **Maybelle Carter** (see page 9) so it's always a good one for showing off your knowledge of two players during the same conversation.

KNOWLEDGEABLE FACT:
His single 'Yakety Axe' was later used on British TV as the 'Benny Hill' theme.

INSTANT OPINION:
The most influential fingerstyle guitarist of all time.

ACCEPTABLE CRITICISM:
Adding CGP to your name is conceited, grandiose and pretentious.

Bob Dylan

HISTORY AND BACKGROUND:
Born Robert Allen Zimmerman, Minnesota, USA, May 24th, 1941. Influenced by 1930s US folkie **Woody Guthrie**, and successfully revived the folk protest song in the mid-1960s. Remained a three-chord acoustic strummer until the mid-60s when he controversially appeared on stage with an electric guitar, prompting booing from assembled folk purists. His guitar playing (and singing) was always immediately recognizable, and many other '60s artists had bigger hits with Dylan songs than the man himself, including **The Byrds** ('Mr Tambourine Man'), **Peter Paul and Mary** ('Blowin' In The Wind') and **Jimi Hendrix** ('All Along The Watchtower').

Bob's still recording and writing, having recently released a compilation of his own songs as well as a new album released to critical acclaim. His own songs are as good as they ever were.

PLAYING STYLE:
Lots of capo'd strumming, but he has had fingerstyle moments too ('Don't Think Twice'). Treats the guitar as vocal accompaniment, hence the approachable level of his technique. Timing is sometimes very loose, reminiscent of his folk, blues and country influences.

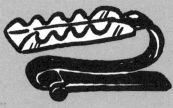

TECHNIQUES TO STEAL:

Fingerstyle, perhaps, but the most important technique we should all learn is to write such good lyrics and memorable songs.

GUITARS:

Over the years has been seen with Martins, Guilds and Gibsons, plus of course that controversial Fender Strat.

ESSENTIAL ALBUM:

For early acoustic hits, check out 1963's *The Freewheelin' Bob Dylan*, but the Dylan album that is standard issue amongst most musicians is 1975's million-selling *Blood On The Tracks*.

FINEST MOMENT:

Loads of 'em... apart from the obvious standards like 'Blowin' in the Wind' and 'The Times They Are a-Changin', 1969's 'Lay Lady Lay' is a four-chord acoustic anthem to make any songwriter weep, and 'Subterranean Homesick Blues' is great to play at your local jam session — if you can remember all the lyrics without cue cards.

KNOWLEDGEABLE FACT:

A bunch of 1970s terrorists named themselves 'The Weathermen' after Dylan's lyric "You don't need a weatherman to know which way the wind blows" from the song 'Subterranean Homesick Blues'.

INSTANT OPINION:

Other people play his songs better than he does.

ACCEPTABLE CRITICISM:

Sings like a vacuum cleaner.

Joni Mitchell

HISTORY AND BACKGROUND:

Born Roberta Joan Anderson in Canada on 7th November 1943. Joni, along with **Chet** and **Bob**, is one of very few acoustic guitarists famous enough to be referred to by first name only. Started playing and singing solo in local coffee bars in the mid-1960s. First album recorded 1967, and by 1969 she was a regular on the Californian hippy-drippy scene. Her song 'Woodstock' was **Crosby, Stills & Nash**'s first single. She's experimented with plenty of different styles over the years, including jazz, rock and choral music, but keeps coming back to her stock in trade — the open-tuned, fingerpicked solo guitar song.

PLAYING STYLE:

Early albums featured very precise, specific fingerstyle parts, which became more strummed and ambiguous on later albums. She has, to date, used 51 tunings, including old favorites like open G and double dropped D, but has also devised many of her own.

TECHNIQUES TO STEAL:

Try making up your own tuning, then making up your own chord shapes, and just see how it sounds. Many of Joni's greatest songs have been written this way. Her early stuff featured non-alternating thumb technique (i.e. you just keep striking the same bass note with the thumb while picking the treble strings).

GEAR:

Generally Martins, but she also owns a Klein custom acoustic, and has recently been using a Roland VG-8 synth guitar system.

ESSENTIAL ALBUM:

For the acoustic parts, go for 1970's *Ladies Of The Canyon*, but the follow-up *Blue* has been bedsit material for hippy student guitarists for over 30 years.

FINEST MOMENT:

'The Priest' from *Ladies Of The Canyon* has a masterful fingerpicked intro using DADGAE tuning, or possibly the intros from early open G songs 'Morning Morgantown' and 'The Circle Game'.

KNOWLEDGEABLE FACT:

Her tunings have been dropping over the years as her vocal range has changed — e.g. 'Big Yellow Taxi' was written in open E, but she now plays it in open C, tuned four half steps lower.

INSTANT OPINION:

She didn't recapture the great acoustic playing of the early material until *Turbulent Indigo* (1994).

ACCEPTABLE CRITICISM:

Some of her more left-field mid-1980s material is tough going for the traditional folkie.

Paul Simon

HISTORY AND BACKGROUND:

Born November 5th, 1941, New Jersey, USA. Got together with singer **Art Garfunkel** while still at school, and had a minor hit in 1957 as teen duo Tom and Jerry. First album *Wednesday Morning 3am* was not a big success, but subsequent 60s albums were huge, including *Sounds Of Silence*, *Bookends* and 1970's *Bridge Over Troubled Water*. After the duo split, solo material moved away from acoustic-based arrangements - in the 1970s and 80s, he plundered reggae ('Mother and Child Reunion'), gospel ('Loves Me Like a Rock'), and South African styles ('Graceland'). Even so, he could always cut it as a straight guitar-vocalist — the 1982 Simon & Garfunkel concert in Central Park contained some great acoustic picking. His songs are still campfire and folk club perennials, and the picking intro from 'The Boxer' still flummoxes the majority of players.

PLAYING STYLE:

Mainly straight fingerstyle in standard tuning ('Homeward Bound', 'Scarborough Fair'), frequently with capo, but he's also written some pretty nifty rhythm parts (the intro to 'Mrs Robinson' or the backing from 'Me And Julio Down By The Schoolyard').

TECHNIQUES TO STEAL:

Many fingerstyle players get by with only three or four right hand patterns, but Paul uses dozens. If you can train your fingers to play so many variations, people will actually start to think your fretted parts are more complex than they really are. Foolproof!

GEAR:

Yamaha custom, Ovation, Gurian, Guild and of course Martin.

ESSENTIAL ALBUM:

The one with the most prominent acoustic guitar playing is probably *Live Rhymin'* (1974) because it's got all the hits on it and Paul plays throughout. *Bookends* is also a great example of how his playing can take on folk, pop and jazz influences.

FINEST MOMENT:

Although the simple 3/4 picking from 'Scarborough Fair' is not difficult to play once you've mastered the thumb part, it's an amazing sound considering that he's just using standard tuning and a capo. Learn it — but don't let anyone see how easy the chord shapes are.

KNOWLEDGEABLE FACT:

Hundreds of artists have recorded his songs, including **Joan Baez**, **Shawn Colvin**, and **Davey Graham** (whose instrumental 'Anji' was recorded by Paul, and who himself later covered 'Bridge Over Troubled Water' and 'Homeward Bound').

INSTANT OPINION:

The best folk-rock songwriter of the 1960s.

ACCEPTABLE CRITICISM:

Plays his own recordings in the background when he holds parties at his house.

Jimmy Page

HISTORY AND BACKGROUND:
Born 9th January 1944, London.
Started playing guitar aged 14.
Worked as a session player
in the 1960s before joining
the **Yardbirds**, then formed
Led Zeppelin in 1968. Despite
the band's electric blues-rock
hits, he also contributed some
stunning acoustic playing,
using many open tunings and
a variety of picking styles.
In post-Zep years, he's worked
with Paul Rodgers of **Free** and
Whitesnake's David Coverdale,
and is currently back with
Robert Plant, a collaboration
which began in true old-men-
of-rock style at a 1994 MTV
unplugged session.

PLAYING STYLE:
Lots of straight fingerstyle, but he is never afraid to go in the other
direction and strum the life out of the instrument. Often takes a simple
two or three note riff and plays it in different rhythmic ways to add
interest. 80% of tunings include DADGAD, open G (DGDGBD) and open
C6 (CACGCE). He's not a perfectionist, often leaving mistakes in on
recordings — some of his meter changes may or may not be intentional!
Has been seen using thumbpick, pick and fingers, or just fingers.

TECHNIQUES TO STEAL:
Keep one open string ringing on while you slide an octave shape
around the fingerboard, strumming all six strings and muting any that
you're not using. This is the classic Page acoustic sound. He's referred
to this as his 'CIA' connection — Celtic, Indian and Arabic.

GEAR:

Most of the early Zeppelin stuff was done on a Harmony acoustic, until he got a Martin D-28 in the early '70s, but he also uses (deep breath) a Yamaha acoustic; a 1920s Cromwell 'cello guitar; a Vega 5-string banjo; a Gibson A4 mandolin; a '60s 'Everly Brothers' black Gibson flat top given to him by **Ron Wood**; a Gibson '20s harp guitar with sympathetic strings; and a small-bodied 12-string Teardrop-shaped acoustic with a cutaway.

ESSENTIAL ALBUM:

Led Zep III is regarded as the band's most 'acoustic' album — check out 'Friends' (weird and Indian) 'Tangerine' (strummy 12-string), and 'Going To California' (multi-layered acoustics).

FINEST MOMENT:

It has to be 'The Rain Song' — loads of jazz voicings in DGCGCD tuning, using a pick and some flatpicking. It's such an unusual guitar part that it even works if you try it without the vocal line.

KNOWLEDGEABLE FACT:

The solo album *Outrider* (1988) was originally written and partly recorded as an acoustic project, but the master tapes were stolen, so he had to start again, and the second version was predominantly electric. This 'lost album' has, of course, since become surrounded in rune-clad mystery and myth among fans.

INSTANT OPINION:

Kula Shaker would never have existed without Jimmy Page.

ACCEPTABLE CRITICISM:

Robert Plant's voice isn't what it was, and recent albums lack some of the energy that early Led Zep stuff had.

Django Reinhardt

HISTORY AND BACKGROUND:

Django was born into a gypsy family — his father worked as a travelling show entertainer. Originally learned banjo and violin. A caravan fire in 1928 damaged his hand, and while he recovered his gypsy friends loaned him a guitar. His third and fourth fingers were locked at the first joint due to the fire, so he could use them for basic chord shapes only — he then developed the two-finger lead style which was his trademark. The famous Quintet du Hot Club de France was formed in 1934 and featured Django and violinist **Stephane Grapelli** as part of a line-up of three guitars, bass and fiddle. The Quintet had international success until 1939. Django travelled Europe and the USA throughout the war, settling down in the late 1940s to record his biggest hit 'Nuages'. Died in 1953, having suffered a brain hemorrhage.

PLAYING STYLE:

High-speed (acoustic) single-note runs and arpeggios (with or without bends), punctuated with partial chord stabs.

TECHNIQUES TO STEAL:

Set up a swing groove at a high tempo (200 BPM+) and play arpeggiated swing eighth notes over it — if you can!

GEAR:

Selmer-Maccaferri acoustic with characteristic 'D' shaped soundhole, although he also played a borrowed archtop f-hole acoustic for one post-war tour. Added a pickup to the Maccaferri later, and went fully electric in 1950.

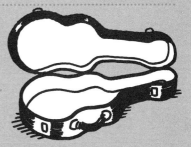

ESSENTIAL ALBUM:

Any *Quintet du Hot Club de France* compilation is essential listening. For maximum cred, try some of his really late recordings (early 1950s) — he's just starting to get into bop.

FINEST MOMENT:

You should learn 'Nuages' note-for-note anyway because it's such a technique-fest. Many players feel he's at his best when performing standards, adding fun and astonishing ideas to established classics. Check out his versions of 'Sweet Georgia Brown' and 'Ain't Misbehavin'.

KNOWLEDGEABLE FACT:

Although he's best-known for the European Hot Club material, Django also worked with big American names such as **Duke Ellington**, **Glenn Miller** and **Dizzy Gillespie** during the 1940s.

INSTANT OPINION:

"Reinvented jazz for Europe".

ACCEPTABLE CRITICISM:

Bien sûr, you are joking, n'est pas?

Emergency backup bluffs

Here are some condensed catalogues on a further eight players, just in case you need additional reference to prove your depth of knowledge.

1. Lonnie Johnson

New Orleans acoustic jazz-blues artist. First recorded under his own name as a guitarist as early as 1925 ('Mr Johnson's Blues'). Duetted with **Eddie Lang**, who used the pseudonym **Blind Willie Dunn**. Pioneered acoustic 12-string as a solo jazz instrument (while Leadbelly did the same for the instrument in Country-Blues). Very firm, tough flatpicking style, on a Grunewald 12-string and Gibson J100. Practically invented the acoustic jazz guitar solo.

2. Robert Johnson

Seminal 1930s bluesman. Extensive use of open tunings, including open G and open A with or without capo. Slide and fingerstyle player. Played slide with bottleneck or knife. Guitars included Gibson L1, Stella and Kalamazoo models. Died in 1938, almost certainly murdered. Influenced dozens of acoustic and electric blues players.

3. Martin Carthy MBE

Legendary folkie, with one of the longest careers of any acoustic guitarist (first album 1965, and still recording). Inspired **Paul Simon** and **Bob Dylan** in the mid-'60s. As well as 22 solo albums, has played in **Steeleye Span**, **The Albion Band**, **The Watersons** and **Brass Monkey**.

Has done more to bring traditional folk music to the foreground than any other British player. Plays a Martin — well, he would, wouldn't he?

4. James Taylor

US singer/songwriter and guitarist — author of many a singalong classic including 'Fire and Rain' and 'Sweet Baby James', and also recorded successful cover of **Carole King**'s 'You've Got a Friend'. Plays fingerstyle in standard tuning or occasionally dropped D, usually with capo. Uses single open chord shapes but complex picking parts.

Notoriously melancholic voice — it's been said that he could sing the phone book and make it sound mournful.

5. Nick Drake

British singer-songwriter and acoustic martyr. Recorded only three albums before he died of an overdose aged 26. Untutored guitarist — made up tunings specifically for songs, used unorthodox fingerpicking techniques. Last album 'Pink Moon' was purely acoustic guitar and voice — the tapes were sent to the record company by mail.

It's extremely fashionable to like Nick Drake these days, so do get hold of some of his stuff.

6. Michael Hedges

American acoustic guitar virtuoso. Used many unusual tunings, including BADEAB and DAEEAA, and applied advanced techniques such as two-handed tapping, hitting the instrument with palms and knuckles, fretted and open harmonics.

Recorded with a regular acoustic, but also used 11- and 17-string harp guitars. Died in a car accident in 1997, aged 43.

7. Suzanne Vega

US singer/songwriter and guitarist, partly responsible for 1980s revival of interest in female acoustic singer-songwriters — since then we've had **Shawn Colvin**, **Beth Orton** and **Jewel**, among others.

These are really now the only artists keeping acoustic guitar songwriting in the album charts, apart from the old guard of ex-rockers on the MTV circuit. Uses a thumbpick and fingers, generally in standard tuning, with capo. Favors sus2 chords which gives much of her early material a spaced-out, ethereal sound.

8. Nick Harper

British singer/songwriter and player. Son of **Roy Harper**. Plays a Lowden fitted with banjo pegs which allows him to incorporate bizarre tuning changes and bent harmonics into a song. First full-length album *Seed* was primarily acoustic. Follow-up *Smithereens* half-electric, half-acoustic, but used the same banjo peg fingerstyle techniques.

Uses tunings such as open G and DADGAD, but dropped by up to four whole steps into 'baritone' guitar range. Heavily influenced by **Jimmy Page**.

Bluffer's Chords or
Easy chord shapes with really complex names

In this section you'll find some of the acoustic bluffer's most essential chords. You know the ones — those ringing, heavenly chords that sound great on intros or as picked accompaniment through loads of reverb.

Most of the time they're achieved simply by placing a simple shape somewhere on the fingerboard and letting some open strings ring on. Not only do they all sound great, they're particularly good for impressing other players, when you casually say something like "oh, that? It's just a D♭maj13♯9♭5."

And remember that however strange a chord sounds, there's always a name for it: strum all the open strings in standard tuning and you get A dominant 9 (no 3) in second inversion, or E minor 11 (no 9) in root position.

'Star Man'

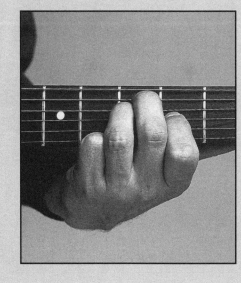

Fmaj7♯11

Fmaj7♯11 (third inversion)
This is the chord that **David Bowie** strums in the fade-in intro to 'Star Man'. Some players put the first finger on the first fret of the sixth string to make a 'normal' Fmaj7♯11.

David Bowie probably didn't use the words "Fmaj7♯11 third inversion" when he wrote the classic 'Star Man' — more likely he said

'Thunder and Lightning'

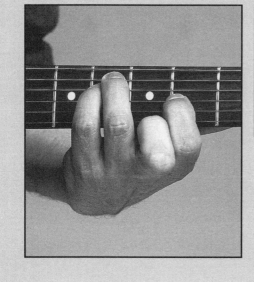

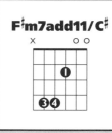

F#m7add11/C#

F#m7add11/C#

It's probably not what **Noel Gallagher**, and **Paul Weller** would call it, but this F#m substitute sounds great on acoustic. It most famously appears in **Thunderclap Newman**'s rock classic 'Something In The Air'.

'Luka'

Bsus4

B sus 4

This is the second in the four-chord sequence which makes up the verse of this **Suzanne Vega** song. The doubled fretted/open B note creates a 12-string effect.

'Wild Wood'

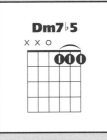

Dm7♭5

Dm7♭5

Paul Weller strums this chord with a capo at the 2nd fret in the title track of his album 'Wild Wood'. The whole song just loops open chord shapes of Am, Em (with A in the bass), Dm, then Dm7♭5, before returning to the Am.

'Dream On'

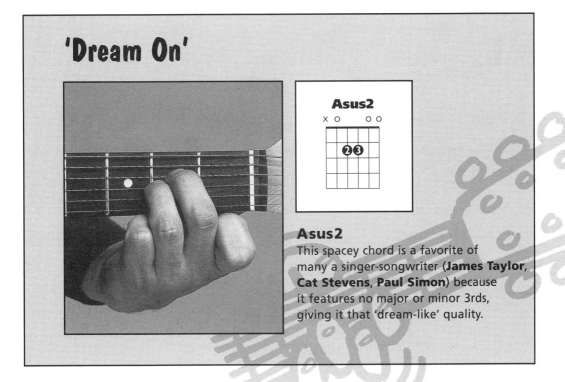

Asus2

Asus2

This spacey chord is a favorite of many a singer-songwriter (**James Taylor**, **Cat Stevens**, **Paul Simon**) because it features no major or minor 3rds, giving it that 'dream-like' quality.

In the 1970s, folk-rockers such as **James Taylor** kept open chords alive — with a capo!

'Fire and Rain'

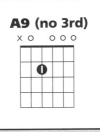

A9 (no 3rd)

A9 (no 3rd)
Sounds great after a straight A7 chord, as used by **James Taylor** at the end of each chorus of 'Fire & Rain'.

'The Pretenders'

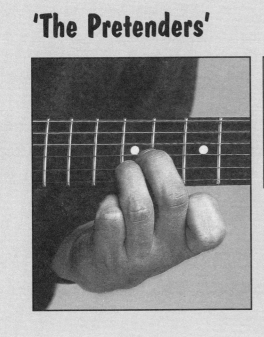

Dadd9 (no 5th)
7 fr

Dadd9 (no 5th)
Although this was played on an electric guitar in **The Pretenders**' song 'Back On The Chain Gang', it's a big favorite with acoustic players too. It works equally well whether strummed or picked.

It's Easy to Fake...
Music and TAB Guide

Most guitar players can't read music. There. We've said it. So you can stop feeling guilty about it and get on with the serious business of pretending that you can. On these two pages you'll find tab and treble clef notation for all of the techniques featured in this book, along with tips on how to play them.

HOW TO READ TREBLE CLEF: The note on the bottom line of the treble clef is middle E — that is, it's the E which is found on the 2nd fret of the D string. The top line is F (1st fret, high E string).

Guitar notes that are lower or higher than this range are notated using 'leger lines' — these are extra staff lines drawn above or below the main clef.

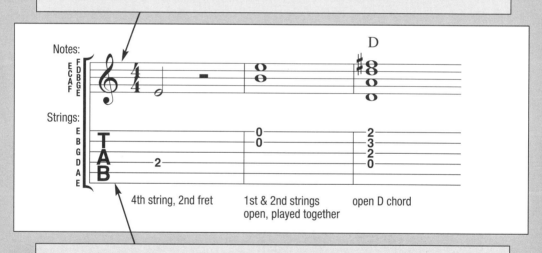

4th string, 2nd fret   1st & 2nd strings open, played together   open D chord

HOW TO READ TAB: The six lines represent the strings — the thickest (lowest) string is on the bottom. The number shows the fret.

HOW TO READ CHORD PARTS: The chord names are written above, and sometimes the musical rhythm of the part is notated underneath.

If no rhythm is given, or you see several even 'slashes' in a bar, then normally you should make up your own rhythm pattern. If you see two chords in a bar, it's normally assumed that they're played for two beats each.

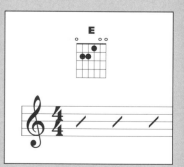

HALF-STEP BEND:
Play the note with the picking hand then bend it up a half step (so it reaches the pitch of the note on the next fret).

WHOLE-STEP BEND:
Duh! Just bend it further!

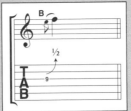

GRACE NOTE BEND:
The only difference with these is that you start bending as soon as you've picked the note. You should hardly hear the first note.

QUARTER-STEP BEND:
Just bend the string a little — don't go as far as a half step. Quarter-step is used to mean any bend that's less than a half step.

BEND AND RELEASE:
Play the note, bend it up, let it back down again.

PRE-BEND:
Bend the note up before you play it.

PRE-BEND AND RELEASE: Bend the note up, then play it, then release the bend while the note rings on.

VIBRATO:
Move the string up and down by rapidly bending and releasing it by a small amount.

HAMMER-ON:
Pick one note, then sound the higher note by fretting it without re-picking. Hammer-ons are always ascending in pitch.

PULL-OFF: Get both fingers into the positions shown in the tab, then pick the higher note. While it rings on, pull the finger off the string to sound the lower note.

SLIDE/GLISS:
While the note is sounding, slide the fretting finger up or down to the position shown in the tab.

SLIDE/GLISS AND RESTRIKE:
As before, but this time repick the second note after you've finishing sliding.

TAPPING: Fret the note using the picking hand by tapping onto the position shown. Usually followed by a pull-off.

PALM MUTING:
Rest the picking hand on the strings very near to the bridge. This partially mutes the notes — the technique is used a lot in blues and rock rhythm playing.

A7/E

SLASH CHORDS:
Many players get confused when they see chord notation like this for the first time. Do not fear — it's simple. The letter name before the slash is the chord you play. The one after the slash is the bass note. Faking tip — if you find it too difficult to play a particular bass note at the same time as the chord, try ignoring it and just playing the chord, then get a bassist or keyboard player to supply the bottom end.

Bert Jansch — responsible for some of the most fiendish folk picking parts of the 1960s.

Rhythm and Picking Patterns or 'Flash don't make cash'

If you have to fake your way through a whole acoustic gig, you'll need to convince everyone in the band that you know your 'rhythm chops', so it's vital that you can play some basic accompaniment styles. In this section you'll find five rhythm parts and five picking patterns, in progressive order of difficulty, which guitarists use when accompanying vocalists or other soloists.

Foolproof Acoustic Rhythm

- When you're playing strummed chord parts, keep the hand moving up and down in an even 8- or 16-to-the-bar pattern, and don't hit the strings at certain points simply to create rhythmic gaps in the part. If you try to stop your hand moving to create gaps, the part won't flow evenly.
- **For subtle, precise rhythm playing, strums should pivot from the wrist. For big, ringing open chord parts, try pivoting from the elbow.**
- Most of the time, you'll get the fullest sound by strumming directly over the soundhole.
- **If you're not using a pick, strum with the backs of the nails on the downstrokes, and with the thumbnail on the upstrokes.**
- If you find that you're using lots of bar chords on a simple acoustic part, try using a capo where the bar would be — it sounds more musical.

Foolproof Acoustic Picking

- The most common mistake people make when they start to learn fingerstyle is to miss the strings with the picking hand. Try anchoring your hand, either by resting the palm on the bridge, or putting your little finger on the body next to the soundhole.
- **Generally, use your thumb on the three bass strings and the first, second and third fingers on the three treble strings.**
- There are three methods of picking — fingers only, pick and fingers ('hybrid picking') or thumbpick and fingers. Bear in mind that if you use hybrid picking, you can't use your first finger on the treble strings.
- **When learning a new fingerstyle part, practice it over and over using just one chord until your fingers 'learn' the rhythm and can do it automatically.**
- Develop the ability to play every thumb-picked and finger-picked note at the same volume — don't let stronger fingers dominate the picking part.

'Bigger Is Better'

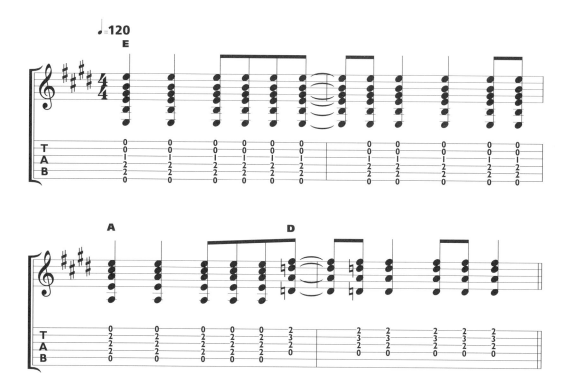

This big, bold strumming pattern gives an all-encompassing 'wall of sound' which is equally at home in a folk club or in a stadium rock band. Use wide, relaxed strumming, and you'll undoubtedly come across as a confident master of all things acoustic.

 # For example

Have a listen to the acoustic work on **The Beatles**' 'While My Guitar Gently Weeps' to hear this technique in action.

'Chakachang!'

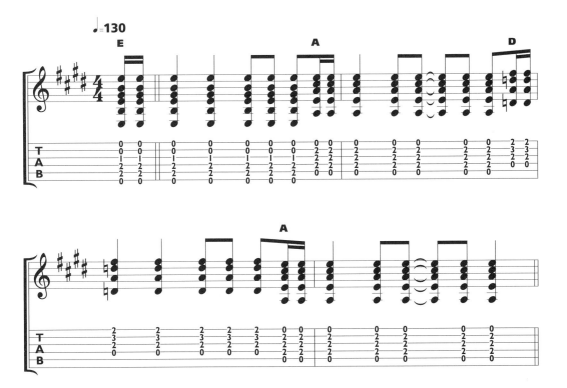

This rhythmic device features a 'pickup' beat, played as two quick strums (down then upstroke) before the main pattern gets going. To assert the full power and majesty of your acoustic accompaniment, use this idea at each chord change.

This popular accompaniment style featured on **Led Zeppelin**'s 'Tangerine' and **The Beatles**' 'Things We Said Today'.

'Wrist and Shout'

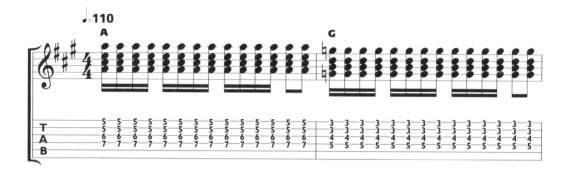

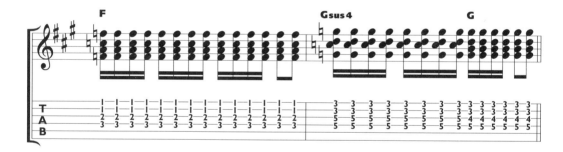

Here's a busy, heavily strummed pattern consisting almost entirely of sixteenth notes. To avoid sounding 'wooden', try varying the strumming attack and accent throughout. Whack the last two beats with wild abandon!

For more ideas, check out **Pete Townshend**'s acoustic on the Who's 'Pinball Wizard', or **Justin Hayward**'s open C-tuned 12-string on The Moody Blues' 'Question'.

'Party 16'

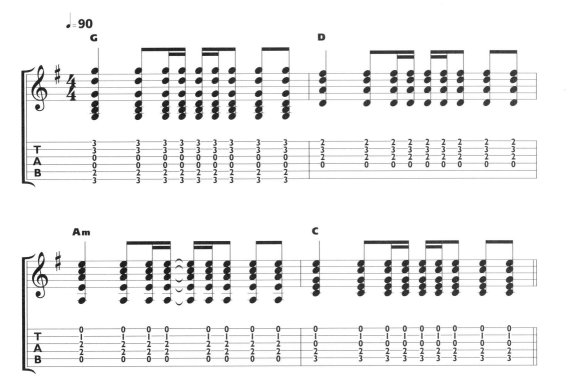

This '90s-style accompaniment rhythm is used by dozens of pop artists, from **Sheryl Crow** to **Oasis**. For a more 'Manchester' type sound, add a little swing to the sixteenth-note beats.

This style could prove very useful at parties, especially if anyone has the audacity to claim they don't want to sing 'American Pie'!

'Rhythm Takes the Lead'

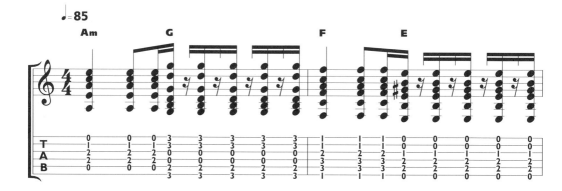

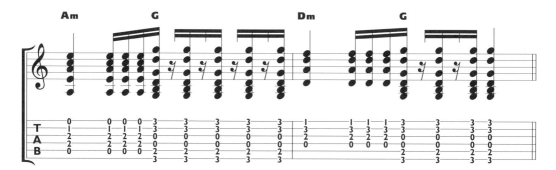

Sometimes an up front acoustic rhythm part can assume as much importance as the drums, or be the sole accompaniment to a vocal.

This pattern demonstrates how a chordal rhythm part can cross over almost into 'riff' territory. At a slower tempo, this is reminiscent of **America**'s 'Horse With No Name'.

'Basic Picking'

This arpeggiated chord pattern is pretty much the 'industry standard'.

There are lots of possible variations to the basic theme, and this example shows how you would transfer the picking pattern to different open chords, always keeping the root note at the bottom. The last two bars showcase just the ascending part of the arpeggio, a popular folk/country trick.

'Feeling All White'

Apparently, **Donovan** showed **The Beatles** this technique in India around 1967. Consequently you'll find the basic pattern all over the *White Album* — take a listen to 'Julia', 'Happiness is a Warm Gun', and 'Dear Prudence' for examples.

Due to the simultaneous root/top notes at the beginning of each bar, this example is best played fingerstyle, with or without a thumbpick.

'Showing Off for No Apparent Reason'

This ascending pattern can be played very quickly indeed once you know the thumb part.

As such, it makes for an excellent bluff when faced with the typical rock accusation that you're playing acoustic because your technique's not fast enough!

'Trumpley Chigwick'

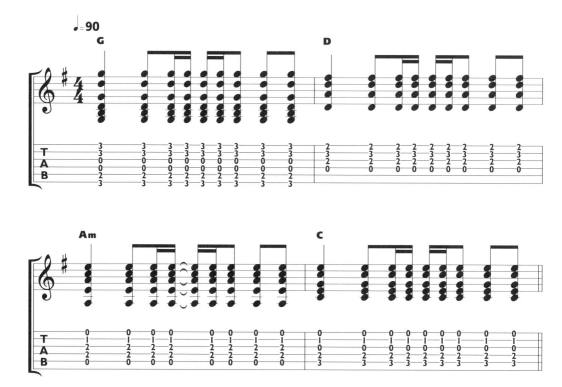

As with most of these patterns, this example is based around the principle of thumb for the three bass strings, with the index, middle and ring finger covering the top three.

Again, this is a standard technique, but you might perhaps recognize a little of the 'Clock' theme from 'Trumpton' there somewhere.

'The Hidden Claw'

One essential skill to develop is your fingers' ability to pluck three strings at once.

After the initial plucked chord, the same notes are arpeggiated — i.e. played one by one. Bar 3 shows the chord changes in half time (for a hint of **Ralph McTell**), followed by the simplest of endings.

Noel Gallagher's four-chord strum-fest 'Wonderwall' became

Musical Examples or 'Don't let them see your fingers or they'll find out how easy it is...'

In this section you'll find 16 musical phrases in progressive order of difficulty, giving an overview of all the common techniques used by acoustic players. Some of them feature a capo, but can be played without if you don't own one.

The one thing that all of these examples have in common is that they sound more difficult than they really are. And let's face it, if you're trying to impress them at your local acoustic jam session, that's what really counts...

Make It Look Difficult

Five easy tricks to make people think you're better than you really are.

- Use a capo really high up (6th-11th fret). The simplest picked chord part sounds more difficult because people are less used to hearing the higher-sounding chords.
- **Remember, any simple picking part played on a 12-string sounds more complicated because of the octave strings. Yes, I know it hurts!**
- Learn two or three syncopated fingerstyle patterns at really high speed. You'll be surprised at how relatively little effort is needed to play a comfortable fingerstyle pattern at a fast tempo.
- **Use a combination of fingerpicking and hammer-ons (with the fretting hand). Never fails.**
- Try to figure out chord shapes which use open strings combined with really high fretted notes. Then try fingerpicking them.

'Alternative Country?'

The country feel of this one is influenced by **Chet Atkins** and **Merle Travis**. This is an 'alternating' bass pattern and can be played with or without a pick.

 **Bluffer's Tip**

If you want to flat pick this riff use only down strokes and keep the attack nice and even. If you are fingerpicking, use your thumb for the bass notes, with index middle and ring fingers chiming out the top line.

'Plectrum Fingerstyle?!'

Once you enter the realms of fingerstyle/flatpicking, the acoustic guitar has infinite possibilities. This riff will project better with a pick. Think of **George Harrison**'s playing on 'Here Comes The Sun', where the acoustic guitar could carry the whole track — including the vocal melody — with no accompaniment whatsoever!

This is a great way to impress other players with a minimum of effort.

'Babe I'm Gonna Pick You'

Most suitable for fingerstyle or fingers with a thumbpick, this riff features
a pattern similar to 'Babe I'm Gonna Leave You', from the first **Led Zeppelin**
album. With the exception of bar three, the arpeggiated chords are arranged in
an ascending pattern throughout.

'All the Wrong Chords'

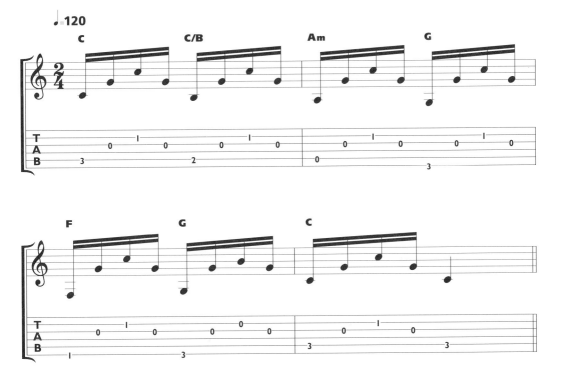

This brisk two-to-the-bar pattern demonstrates the freedom fingerstyle playing can provide from traditional chord voicings/fingerings.

The first fret of the second string is held throughout, while the bass note moves to imply different harmonies every beat. Though taking its origins from the classical guitar, this is a must in every acoustic bluffer's arsenal.

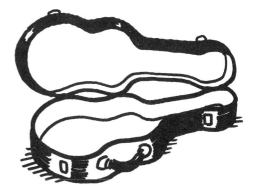

'Bob's Clawhammer'

If you incorporate hammer-ons into a pattern which uses a finger 'claw' technique, it's called — you guessed it — clawhammer technique. This example is influenced by early Country and American folk-blues, which was later taken on board by **Donovan** and **Bob Dylan**.

The chord changes in this style of music don't need to follow the same 'rules' as far as timing goes. Bob would often hold on to a chord for an extra beat, or change earlier in the bar than you may expect.

'Protest Too Much'

Moving forward a few decades, here is a clearer example of the **Dylan**/protest song style. Usually played with a pick, Bob would usually stick with open chords and use a capo to change key for different songs.

Again, watch the third bar for a demonstration of the 'freetime' approach, which will endear you to dyed-in-the-wool folkies and blues dudes alike.

'Carter Picking'

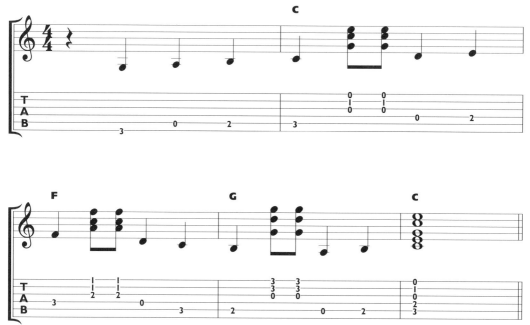

This example demonstrates how you can create the illusion of two guitars playing at once by playing the tune in the bass and strumming the top few strings in the gaps between notes, as popularized by 1930s Country band **The Carter Family**.

Using a capo at a higher register can give a banjo-like effect.

'Droning On and On About India'

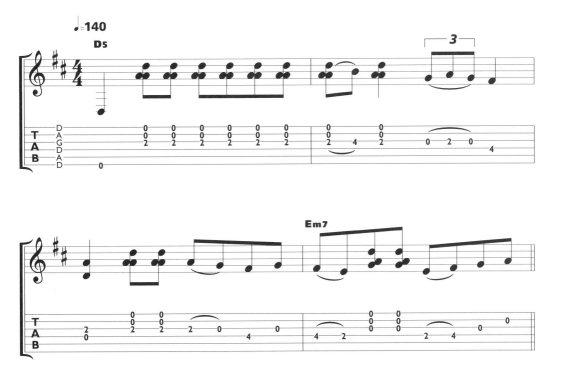

Here's our first example in a tuning (see page 77) — this one uses DADGAD. The riff itself keeps things moving, while the open strings act as a drone, or pedal note.

Apparently based on a sitar tuning, it's easy to hear the Indian heritage if you try sliding single notes or octaves around the neck, **Jimmy Page**/**Nick Harper** style. The last bar hints at the 'banjo roll' technique favored by country players.

'Sliding a Broom'

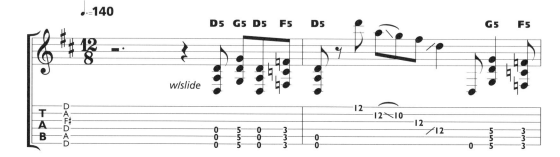

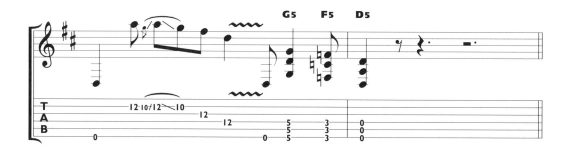

This typical bottleneck/slide pattern uses open D tuning (as in **Elmore James'** version of the blues standard 'Dust My Broom'). Open tunings are probably the biggest secret of slide playing, as they allow whole or partial chords to be played using only the slide.

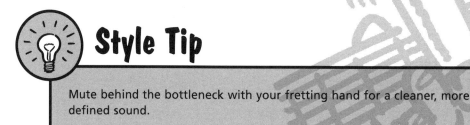

Style Tip

Mute behind the bottleneck with your fretting hand for a cleaner, more defined sound.

'Little Ben'

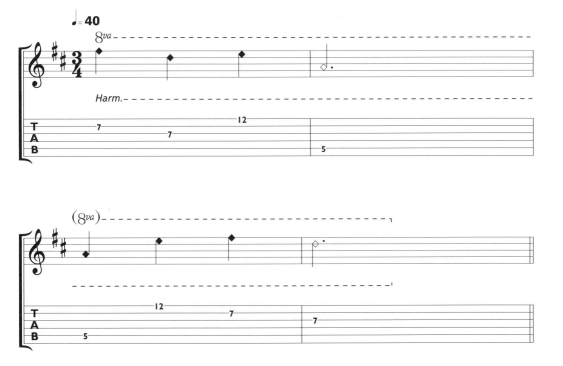

Okay, so this one isn't all that difficult, but it does demonstrate how melodies can be played using harmonics exclusively. This 'Big Ben Chimes' example is only the beginning.

To hear this technique being taken further, check out 'Horizons' from **Steve Hackett**'s acoustic album *Bay of Kings*.

'Hedgerow of Harmonics'

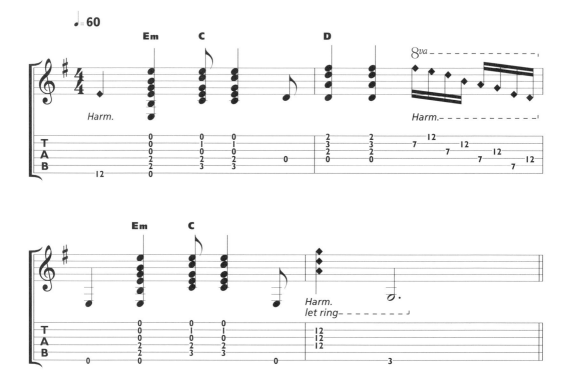

Incorporating natural harmonics into a riff gives an impressive effect, without having to make a supreme amount of effort.

During the second bar, ripple out these **Michael Hedges**-style harmonics at the 7th and 12th frets, jumping seamlessly back into the main riff. To finish, the 12th fret harmonics are superimposed over a low E, then G, to give your listeners an extra surprise!

'Rollin' Banjos'

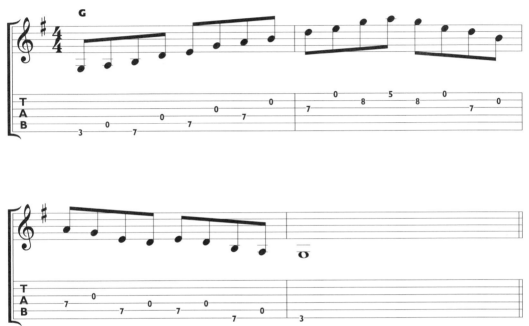

This example of a banjo roll technique combines open and fretted notes to produce ringing scalic lines. Famously associated with **Chet Atkins**, the sky is the limit as far as tempo is concerned!

There are lots of opportunities for this kind of playing all over the fingerboard — if you can find them!
Try this approach using open tunings and you'll really stump the tab transcribers in your audience.

'Byrds in the Hand'

This bluegrass style lick is based around the style of **Clarence White**.

Entirely in open position, it features two different parts. It starts with a descending scale pattern with repeated open string pedal tones, followed by a chromatic alternate-picked line in the last two bars.

This will take some practice, but will earn you the respect of even the most cynical acoustic expert.

The legendary **Clarence White** — the grand-daddy of open-position flatpicking.

'Harping On'

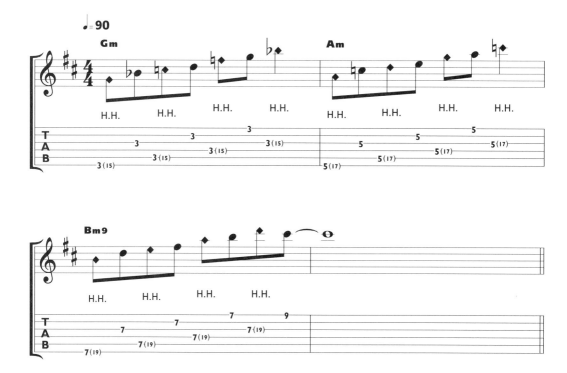

Once you've mastered the technique required to fret and pluck the harmonic simultaneously, be prepared to receive admiring glances from other players, who will wonder exactly how you are doing it.

You should keep your back to these people, naturally. Unless they've got a copy of this book too...

'Acousto-Electric'

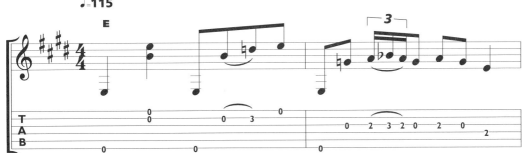

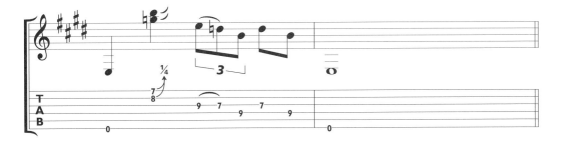

This example shows how acoustic players can borrow electric guitar techniques and adapt them for their own style.

Here, the bluesy quarter-tone bends should work even with heavy strings, and the hammer-ons are really just there as an aid to speed.

The late **Michael Hedges** — a modern-day virtuoso of the acoustic guitar.

'Easy and Mellow'

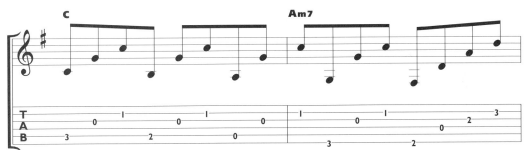

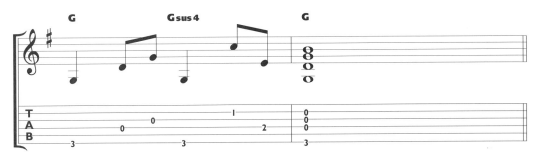

Based in the key of G, this fingerstyle workout spends the first four bars using a **Beatles**/**Donovan** picking style, which shifts up a gear for a descending sequence in bars 7 and 8. This is a classic **Beatles** songwriting device. The Gsus4 chord in the second half of bar 7 is pure **Eagles**, as in the intro to 'Take It Easy'.

Chord Sequences or "Why does everything I play sound like country?"

When acoustic players try to write songs, their musical ideas are often very 'samey'. This is due to the fact that the open chords we all know and love — G, C, D, Am etc — have been used thousands of times by other songwriters.

In this section, the five chord sequences supplied are designed to break your playing out of such ruts by giving you harmonic ideas from a variety of styles. And if someone does accuse your playing of being predictable, you can always tell them that **Bob Dylan**'s a big influence...

Songwriting Cliché Hell

We all do it - write a new song and it just goes G, Em, C etc... and then we realize we've heard it all before. So just how do you avoid all your own clichés?

- Try a new tuning. Even simple dropped D will give you new ideas for chords.
- **Try a different strumming pattern. Do you** *really* **need to use the right hand part from 'Wonderwall' on everything?**
- Play it slower, or faster. A simple change of tempo will alter the feel of the changes and inspire you differently.
- **Learn a new chord! Do your songs always avoid E♭6 because you don't like the sound of it? Or is it really because you can't play it?**
- If it's strummed, play it fingerstyle. And vice versa.

'Loopy Chords'

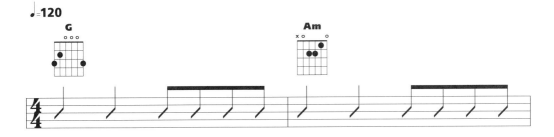

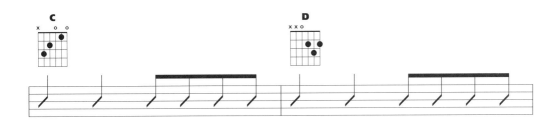

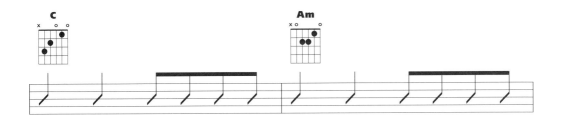

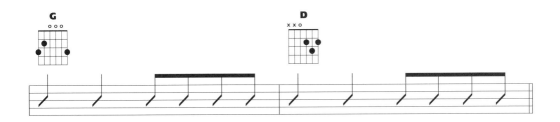

This kind of sequence works played over and over, i.e. the final D chord is the ideal vehicle for leading back to the G chord, where you would begin again. The rhythm notation is here for guidance only — depending on the strumming pattern you chose, this could be effective as straight country, blues, R&B or even reggae!

'Jazz At Five'

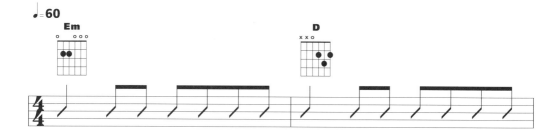

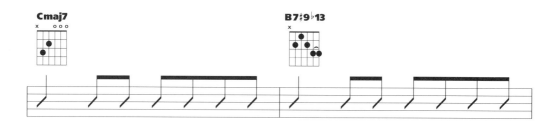

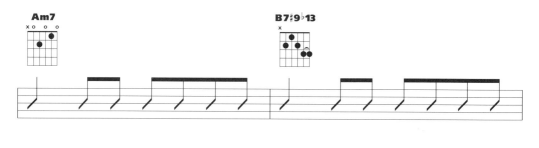

More moody in feel, this E minor based example features a jazzy B7#9♭13 chord, giving a sound reminiscent of songwriter **John Martyn**. The Am7 adds extra detail to the picture, though the temptation to use these jazzy 7ths all the time is a little like leaving a chorus pedal constantly switched on — you can have too much of a good thing!

'Jingle Jangle Morning'

♩=120

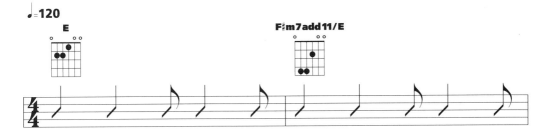

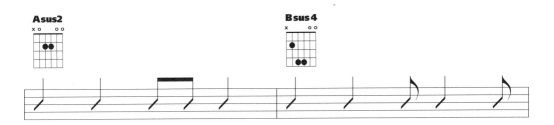

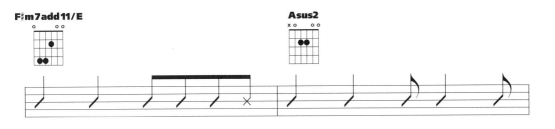

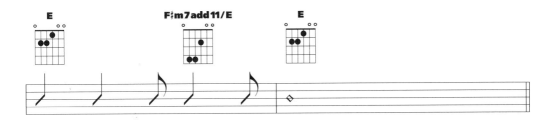

The key to this example is the big-sounding open E voicing — the progression features the first and second strings ringing openly throughout. There are a few rhythmic details added as suggestions, but if you regard this as the big acoustic backing for a country rock song (especially on a 12 string), just sit back and let your strumming arm do the work.

'Acoustic Attitude'

♩=120

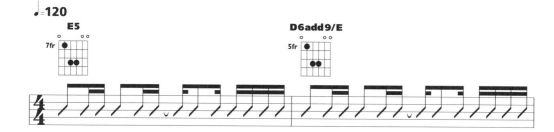

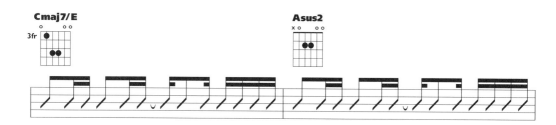

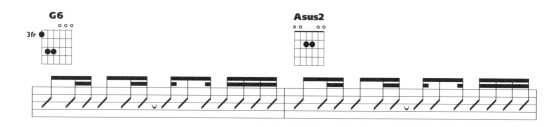

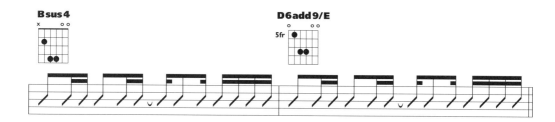

This example has a more dramatic feel, due to the dissonant voicings and frantic strumming pattern. Even raking across the chords slowly, you can feel the tension building, ready to kick back into an acoustic rock feel. This proves acoustic guitars are about more than just picking and grinning!

'Cambric Shirt'

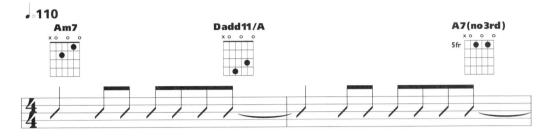

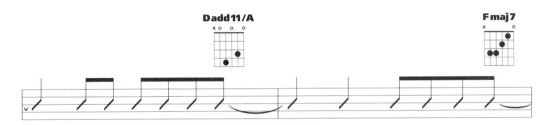

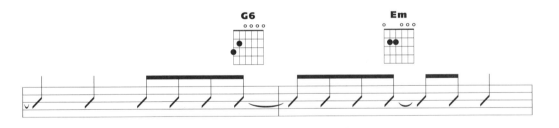

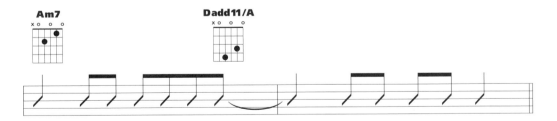

These are actually quite traditional folk chords, especially the ethereal Dadd11/A, which recurs throughout. This sort of voicing features prominently in **Paul Simon**'s arrangement of 'Scarborough Fair' — note that the chords work far better as a picked pattern than as complete strums.

Martin player **Stephen Stills** was a big fan of the EBEEBE tuning — check out his fingerpicked recording '4+20'.

Altered Tunings or "I just don't understand — it was in tune when I got it back from the shop."

One way of avoiding the more obvious clichés of the acoustic guitar is to tune it differently. This can be as simple as altering the bass string to create a low bottom note (The Beatles, Chet Atkins, Stephen Stills) or making up a completely new tuning specifically for the song (Gordon Giltrap, Nick Drake, Paul Simon).

Either way, tunings are a really useful way of coming up with exciting new sounds on the acoustic guitar. In this chapter you'll find five tab examples, each showing a typical usage of that tuning. Tip — the more obscure the tuning, the more you can gleefully annoy other guitarists in the audience who try to figure out what you're playing. And if you use a capo as well you'll probably not make it out of the gig alive...

All The Tunings

Here, I've listed all the other commonly-used alternate tunings for you to try. Don't blame me if you break a string, though!

- **"DOUBLE DROPPED D" DADGBD** Same as open G but without the A string altered.
- **"DROPPED C" CADGBE** Just drop the bottom string two whole steps lower and play a big C major chord.
- **"OPEN D MINOR" DADFAD** Good for English folk.
- **"ALL THE 4THS" EADGCF** Only used by a few jazzers and some 6-string bass players. Difficult.
- **"DADGAE"** A variation on DADGAD, as used by Joni Mitchell.
- **"NASHVILLE" EADGBE** The three bass strings are tuned an octave higher (so you need thinner strings!). Popular in Country, y'all.
- **"LAZY BOTTLENECK" EADGBD** A quick way of tuning your guitar to open G which works for bottleneck lead parts, as long as you don't play the two bass strings.
- **"E♭ TUNING" E♭A♭D♭G♭B♭E♭** The whole guitar, dropped a half step in tuning.
- **BARITONE TUNING** Any tuning (usually regular, dropped D or open G) with all the strings dropped a fourth or a fifth (e.g. regular tuning would become BEADF♯B).

'Dropped D' — DADGBE

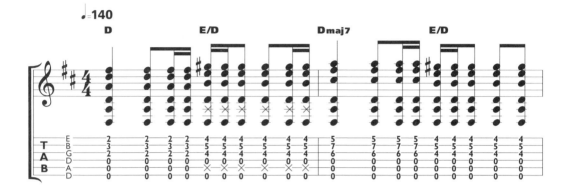

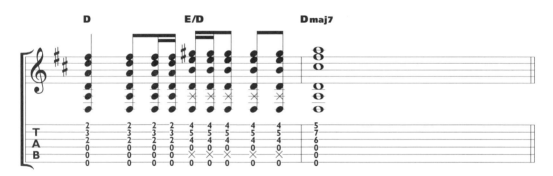

Taking the 6th string down to D gives you lots of freedom with moveable D major/minor chord shapes, as you can leave all six strings ringing all the time.

Of course you may want to save the impact of this low D for a critical moment, as in **Fleetwood Mac**'s 'Oh Daddy'. Using it as a pedal tone under other chords (like A7) can also give pleasant results.

'Open G' — DGDGBD

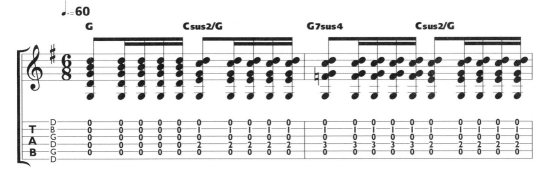

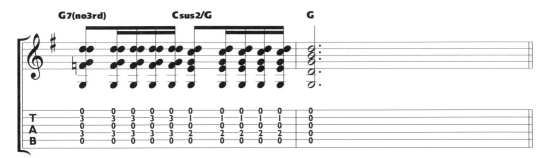

This open G tuning is one of the most popular, and can be heard on recordings by artists as diverse as **The Rolling Stones** and **Gordon Giltrap.** The sixth string — detuned to D — is not often used.

'Open D' — DADF#AD

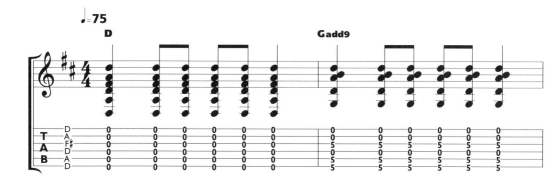

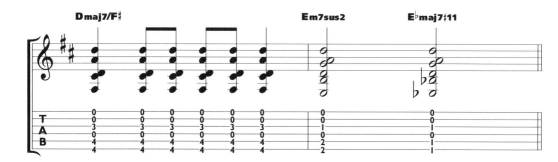

Another popular folk tuning, this open D is along similar lines to the open E used by **Joni Mitchell** in 'Big Yellow Taxi'.

It lends itself to big, full-sounding strummed chords. Most patterns which work in open G can be transferred across a string for a deeper, more resonant sound.

This tuning can also be heard in action during the acoustic intro of the **Stones'** 'You Can't Always Get What You Want'.

'Open C' — CGCGCE

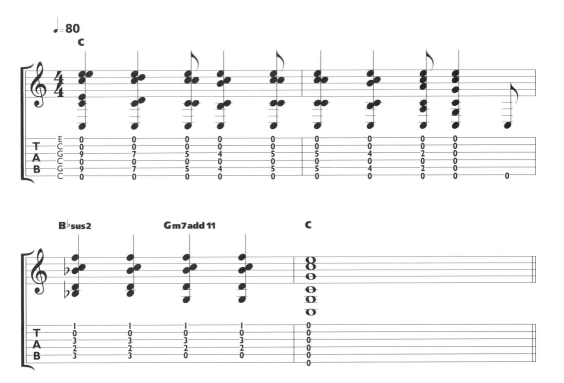

This tuning is great for meandering Indian influenced lines, using the open strings as a sitar-like drone (remember **Jimmy Page**'s 'CIA' connection?).

This example demonstrates a moving octave shape over the C drone, changing to some open position chords which would be totally unplayable in standard tuning. Let it be our secret...

'Dad-Gad' — DADGAD

If you're a **Zeppelin** fan, this tuning suggests 'Black Mountain Side' and 'Kashmir'. If you prefer the older school of folk guitar playing, think of **Davey Graham** and **John Renbourn**.

Music Shop Classic or 'How do I fit everything in this book into 24 bars of showing off?'

Even the most sullen, gum chewing Saturday assistant breaks into a grimly patronizing scowl at the thought of yet another version of 'Blackbird'. Watch the sharp intake of breath as you launch into the rippling harmonics at the beginning of this specially-designed showcase of your ample ability. This piece has everything a great acoustic guitar solo should — flash-sounding techniques, lots of open strings, and that somehow-heard-it-before quality.

The opening run consists entirely of harmonics, which should be allowed to ring together as much as possible. The chord progression stays mostly around open chord shapes, to maximize opportunites for soloing high up the neck while the open strings ring out.

For the last section, we're moving our fretting hand higher up the neck for some single-note lead playing, with a bluesy quarter-step bend added in for good measure. The dramatic harmonic ending is played in 'free time', giving you a chance to think up clever answers to all the questions the admiring fans around you are bound to ask!

'Influences'

Just so you know who to name-drop when you're describing your 'influences' to the shop assistant, the Music Shop Classic features techniques and ideas taken from:

Adrian Legg, Michael Hedges, Pink Floyd, Neil Young, Nick Harper, Pete Townshend, Mark Knopfler, Jimmy Page.

Hope it gets you a discount!

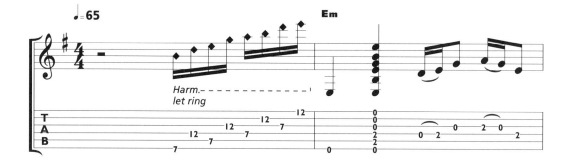

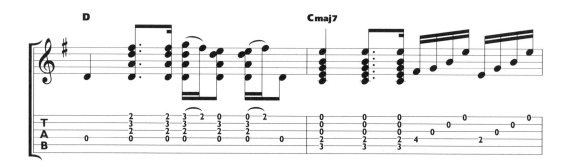

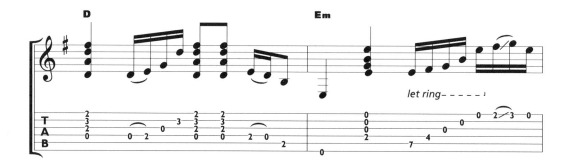

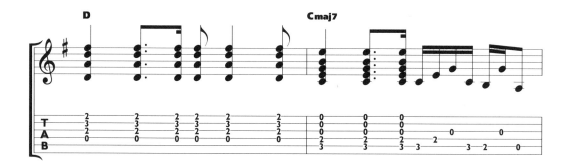

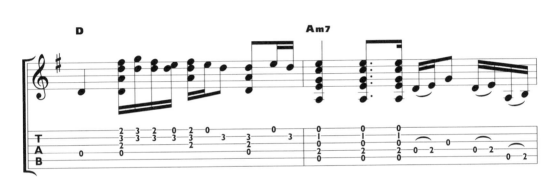

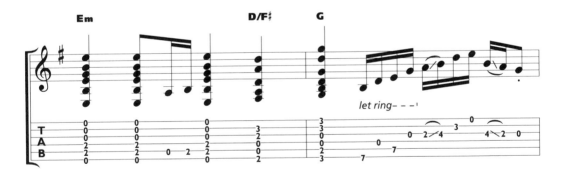

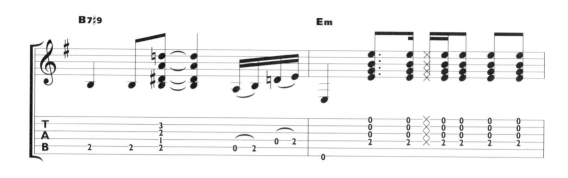

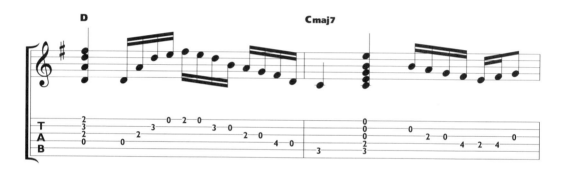

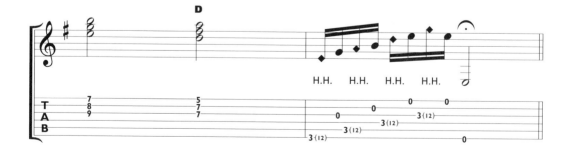

Music Shop Riffs — the dos and don'ts

If you *have* to play party pieces in a music shop, you might as well choose one of the 'standards'. On this page, I've listed some of the most popular acoustic pieces currently being played in music shops.

You can get away with some of them yourself — indeed, several are expected of you — but others will result in laughs of scorn from those in the know. Next to each riff is listed an advisability rating (10 means it's essential repertoire, 1 means you'll be lucky to leave the shop with your nose still attached to your face) and tips on which bit to play.

Title	Artist	Rating	Tips
Anji (aka 'Angie')	Davey Graham	9	You need your fretting hand thumb over the top of the neck to play this tune, but if you can cope with the speed, it's an excellent showpiece. Most people only learn the first two bars and play them endlessly.
St James' Infirmary	Various	8	Great for cementing your Delta Blues credentials. This well-loved minor blues is instant cred.
Alice's Restaurant	Arlo Guthrie	6	The guitar part for this classic '60s talking blues is only 16 bars long (even though the song itself lasts for 18 minutes!). Even so, it's a great fingerstyle part with a nice swing to it.
Wonderwall	Oasis	5	Has the advantage of being (fairly) contemporary, and dead easy to play, but has worn a bit thin with most retailers now. Capo 2nd fret, in case you didn't know.
Hotel California	The Eagles	5	Well-known, but not as clichéd as 'Stairway...'. Go for the fingerstyle intro, but bear in mind that the thumb part isn't a simple alternating 4-to-the-bar.
Streets Of London	Ralph McTell	2	A great song in its time, but forced into cliché hell by too many bad folk club versions. Avoid.
Stairway To Heaven	Led Zeppelin	0	One of only two intros to be banned absolutely by international treaty. (the other being 'Smoke On The Water'). Never, EVER play this song.

Guitars! or
'Surely it's more important to be
a good player?'

More important than technique, hair style, even beard length, is the type of guitar you're seen with. A player can get away with horrendous musicianship if they own an envy-inducing instrument.

The reasoning goes something like this; if you see someone with a guitar which cost more than your house, you get to thinking that they wouldn't have spent all that money unless they could really get the best out of it. All too often, of course, it just means that they've got more cash than you. But admit it, for a second, when you saw that guitar in its case, you thought the owner was a better player, didn't you?

Here, then, is a selection of the guitars to know if you want to command maximum respect among the acoustic community. All usage of jargon has, of course, been maximized for your convenience.

If you're a good player, you can
even get away with one of these!

National/Dobro

DATA:
In modern times, famously appeared on the cover of the 1985 Dire Straits album *Brothers In Arms*. These all-metal or metal-and-wood guitars had a convex bowl at the front to reflect the sound. They came about because of the need to make the acoustic guitar louder (which is why sales dipped when the electric guitar was invented). The National and Dobro brands were basically the same company, but various corporate arguments, law suits and shareholder buyouts led to great confusion about which was which. Nowadays, either word can be used to describe this type of guitar.

FAMOUS NAMES:
Mark Knopfler, Sol Hoopii (famous 1930s Hawaiian player), various bluesmen (Son House, Bukka White, Blind Boy Fuller).

DESIGN:
The bridge is mounted onto a bowl-like aluminium cone, and it's the cone, rather than the whole guitar body, which vibrates. Even though the bowl appears to be directing the sound towards the back of the guitar, the system does seem to work. More expensive models had a complex three-cone arrangement.

SOUND:
Very loud, allegedly 7 times louder than normal acoustic, and on a par with the banjo. Metal cone reflectors give an upper-midrange emphasis that adds to apparent volume.

KNOWLEDGEABLE FACT:
Some models had a squared-off hollow neck, making them suitable for Hawaiian lap slide techniques, but impossible for regular guitar playing.

INSTANT OPINION:
The classic sound for acoustic bottleneck lead playing. And they look soooo cool...

ACCEPTABLE CRITICISM:
Not very versatile outside of blues and Hawaiian styles.

1935 (Dobro) Regal 16M Artist.

Martin D-28

DATA:

This is the original 'Dreadnought' guitar shape, and almost every manufacturer in the world has come up with a similar-looking instrument. (The name, incidentally, comes from the huge 1906 battleship HMS Dreadnought, and refers to the fact that it was the largest Martin guitar). Production model introduced 1931, and still being made today. A vintage D-28 from the early 1930s in good condition can fetch as much as $27,000.

FAMOUS NAMES:

Joni Mitchell, Jimmy Page, Paul Simon, Bob Dylan.

DESIGN:

Spruce top, round soundhole, black pickguard, bound body, ebony fingerboard (old models), rosewood fingerboard (new models).
Basic and uncomplicated.

SOUND:

Due to its large body size, a D-28 gives a rich, deep bass end and a warm midrange. Beware — although a cheap copy may look the same, it will always sound different due to different construction materials.

KNOWLEDGEABLE FACT:

In 1959 Martin brought out an electric version, the D-28E. This curious-looking beast had two pickups, two volume and two tone knobs, and a three-position slider switch. Not popular with the purists!

INSTANT OPINION:

Worth selling your house for. If it's a vintage one, throw your soul into the bargain.

ACCEPTABLE CRITICISM:

No-one's soul is worth that much cash.

!!?#

1940 Martin D-28 with Herringbone Trim.

Ovation

DATA:
Ovation guitars are best-known for their synthetic round backs. Founder Charles H. Kaman initially approached Martin with his revolutionary guitar design ideas, before deciding to start out on his own. First model was the 1967 Balladeer. Still best-sellers, although the synthetic design still worries some traditionalists. Kaman music also owns Takamine guitars.

FAMOUS NAMES:
Glen Campbell, Jimmy Page and Richie Sambora (both twin-neck 6/12 strings), John Williams and Kevin Peak (roundbacked classicals with '70s supergroup Skye), Adrian Legg, Al Di Meola.

DESIGN:
Apart from a flat wood top (it's actually laminate of wood and carbon graphite), the rest of the body is all synthetic. Most models are active electro-acoustic, with a piezo pickup, 3-band EQ and volume control. Distinctive bevelled headstock.

SOUND:
The bowl back reflects a lot of mid and treble, and when plugged in the pickup adds yet more top end. There's not a lot of bass to be had but this can be partly fixed with the tone controls.

KNOWLEDGEABLE FACT:
Charles H. Kaman had a background in helicopter design, forming the Kaman Aircraft Corporation in 1945. The original Ovation prototypes were built by aerospace engineers.

INSTANT OPINION:
The most revolutionary acoustic guitar design this century.

ACCEPTABLE CRITICISM:
When unamplified, the guitars don't have the same rounded warmth as large-bodied wooden acoustics.

1978 Ovation Adamas with fiberglass 'bowl' back.

Unplugged? or
'How loud should I have the amplifier?'

Have you ever watched an 'acoustic set' by any guitar-based artist? Chances are, they're using more technology than the space shuttle program to create their sound. If the acoustic guitar is going to be recorded or amplified, you need to get its sound into an amp or mixing console in some way.

On this page I've shown some tips on amplifying the acoustic guitar, based on the pitfalls that many players experience when they try to play a live acoustic set for the first time.

There are two basic methods — mike up an acoustic guitar, or use one with an on-board pickup. If you want a convenient, consistent sound, I'd strongly recommend the latter. Apart from the fact that microphones are more prone to feedback, peripheral noise, stands falling over etc, they have the added disadvantage that they pick up the sound of your swearing when you hit a bad note...

Strings

- Use new strings if you can afford to — they have more treble and will stay in tune better (once you've stretched them, that is). If you can't afford a new set, clean the existing ones with string cleaner.
- Don't put nickel electric strings on an acoustic guitars. Use bronze or phosphor bronze types.
- Don't be a strings wimp! If your guitar is set up properly, you should be able to play with .012 gauge strings quite comfortably. Some acoustic guitar manufacturers recommend you don't use anything less than a .013 set on their instruments. If your style doesn't involve bending notes, you should be able to go to .014 or even higher. Generally, use the highest gauge you can stand — the guitar will always sound better for it.
- Have your guitar set up to make sure the nut is cut properly. If it's not, you'll have tuning problems, not to mention some pain on the open chord shapes.

Unplugged tips:

Miking up

- Try to use a guitar with a naturally loud sound — this gives the mic more to work with and will ultimately sound less apologetic. Similarly, thicker strings (0.12 and up) will make the body vibrate more, giving you a better/louder tone, and therefore a clearer mic signal.

- If you're using a PA, don't place the mic directly in front of the soundhole! The guitar body will act as an air chamber (as it's designed to) and create bass-end feedback.

- Place the microphone in front of the top few frets instead — close to the soundhole but not so close that you get feedback.

Guitars with pickups

- The most common type of pickup is the 'piezo' — a crystal-based pickup which lives in the bridge of the instrument. These are sometimes too bright-sounding, so you may have to turn down the treble to get the most natural sound.

- Just because it's got a jack lead, it doesn't necessarily follow that you have to use effects pedals. Reverb perhaps, chorus if you must, but really, do you need that multi-tapped flange ring modulation distortion filter?

- Don't plug it into a regular guitar amp — use a PA, keyboard amp or dedicated acoustic combo. Guitar amps have speaker systems which are designed to emphasize the midrange frequencies of the electric guitar. Acoustic guitars benefit from a more natural, pure sound.

Many gigging acoustic guitarists use electro-acoustics such as this Gibson. They don't sound *exactly* like a mic-ed up acoustic, but they sure beat bumping into the mic stand.

Above: 1990 Gibson 'Chet Atkins' SST (steel string) electro-acoustic.

Acoustic light-bulb jokes

Q: How many bluegrass guitarists does it take to change a light bulb?
A: What, you mean this sucker's electric?

Q: How many folk guitarists does it take to change a light bulb?
A: Five — one to change the bulb, and four to sing about how great the old one was.

Q: How many blues guitarists does it take to change a light bulb?
A: You mean the light bulb's gone and left me too?

Q: How many keyboard players who try to imitate acoustic guitar sounds does it take to change a light bulb?
A: Two — one to use a sampler to record the original bulb's light, then another one to paint a picture of a candle and say 'hey, that's just like a real light bulb!'

Q: How many fingerstyle players does it take to change a light bulb?
A: Only one — if you can't do the whole thing on your own, your technique's obviously not up to the job.

Q: How many acoustic jazz guitarists does it take to change a light bulb?
A: Man, I only change my bulbs once every ten years, however dead they get.

Q: How many 12-string guitarists does it take to change a light bulb?
A: Only one, but he needs a couple of hours to get ready.

Q: How many capo-equipped acoustic guitarists does it take to change a light bulb?
A: None. Just move the window up a bit, then you won't be needing any other bulbs.

Q: How many guitar makers does it take to change a light bulb?
A: Ten. **One** to scour the Brazilian rainforest for the perfect piece of glass; a **second** to let the glass dry out for 100 years in oak-aged casks; a **third** to treat it with a special secret resin which can only be obtained by distilling the milk of an Austrian mountain yak; a **fourth** to ensure that the bulb and its holder are perfectly bookmatched so that you can't see any difference between the two; a **fifth** to visit the glaziers to insist on laminated glass rather than that cheap bonded rubbish; a **sixth** to put the glass into a mould of his own design which bears no relation to the design of any other well-known light-bulb manufacturers; a **seventh** to apply decorative edging to the socket; an **eighth** to cut his own socket from animal bone; a **ninth** to make sure the bulb is glued, NOT screwed into the socket; and a **tenth** to line the bulb's box with the finest ermine so that its light-giving subtleties will last well into the next century.

Oh, and we have to keep our guitars in low-light conditions at all times to avoid damaging the perfection of the grain, so we won't be needing that bulb.

Campfire Hell

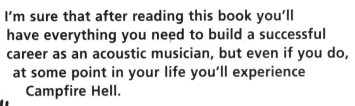

I'm sure that after reading this book you'll have everything you need to build a successful career as an acoustic musician, but even if you do, at some point in your life you'll experience Campfire Hell.

This is where a bunch of players and singers get together late at night and challenge those autocratic and oppressive musical concepts like tuning accuracy, knowing how the song goes and playing the same chords as each other.

If you do get caught in such a situation, it helps to have done some preparation:

Firstly

Learn the entire Beatles back catalogue. That's just under 140 songs, so start with crowd-pleasers like 'Hey Jude' and 'Let It Be' and work your way up to 'The Continuing Story of Bungalow Bill' and 'Revolution #9'. I guarantee you'll be asked to play every Beatles tune at least once in your life.

Secondly

Have at least one classic diddly-dee folk tune at your fingertips (Scarborough Fair, unfortunately, doesn't count because someone's had a hit with it). If you can't start an obscure 'traditional' tune on your own you'll be considered a phoney by the diehards. Don't worry if you don't know one — just improvize a melody in open C and call it 'The Hangman's Gypsy Shanty Mineshaft Disaster' or something. Should fool 'em OK.

Finally

Bring along a capo. It's a sure bet that someone else in the group will have one, so if you're frantically trying to follow their chords, the last thing you need is to be instantly transposing the song as you play. Plus, of course, there's always some dreadful warbling female singer or grunting Johnny Cash impersonator who can't do 'Blackbird' in the original key. Unless you'd rather try and figure it out using bar chords? Thought not.

If you've enjoyed this book, why not check out the other books in this great new series, available from all good music and book retailers, or in case of difficulty, direct from Music Sales (see page 2).

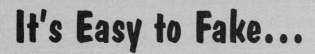

Blues Guitar	Rock Guitar	Acoustic Guitar	Jazz Guitar
AM 973775	AM 973764	AM 973786	AM 973753

JOE BENNETT has been teaching guitar for fifteen years, and regularly works as a session guitarist. He is also a senior examiner in electric guitar for The London College of Music and Head of Popular Music at City of Bath College. Joe's publications include the *Guitar: To Go!* and *Really Easy Guitar* series, and *The Little Book of Scales*, plus tracks and articles for *Future Music*, *PowerOn* and *Total Guitar* magazines.